RUBÁIYÁT OF
OMAR KHAYYÁM

Rubáiyát of Omar Khayyám

RENDERED INTO ENGLISH VERSE BY

EDWARD FITZGERALD

With illustrations by

EDMUND DULAC

DOUBLEDAY

NEW YORK LONDON TORONTO SYDNEY AUCKLAND

PUBLISHED BY DOUBLEDAY

A division of Bantam Doubleday Dell Publishing Group, Inc.
666 Fifth Avenue, New York, New York 10103

DOUBLEDAY and the portrayal of an anchor with a dolphin
are trademarks of Doubleday, a division of Bantam Doubleday
Dell Publishing Group, Inc.

ISBN 0-385-00146-0

PRINTED IN THE UNITED STATES OF AMERICA
DOUBLEDAY EDITION: 1952

30   32   34   35   33   31

TABLE OF CONTENTS

Biographical Preface   11

Omar Khayyám—The Astronomer-Poet of Persia   27

The First Edition of the Translation   41

The Second Edition of the Translation   79

The Fifth Edition of the Translation   135

Variations in the Third Edition of the Translation   187

LIST OF ILLUSTRATIONS

FOLLOWING PAGE 48

The First Edition of the Translation

QUATRAIN I

Awake! for Morning in the Bowl of Night
Has flung the Stone that puts the Stars to Flight:
   And Lo! the Hunter of the East has caught
The Sultán's Turret in a Noose of Light.

QUATRAIN XI

Here with a Loaf of Bread beneath the Bough,
A Flask of Wine, a Book of Verse—and Thou
   Beside me singing in the Wilderness—
And Wilderness is Paradise enow.

QUATRAIN XXIV

Alike for those who for To-DAY prepare,
And those that after a To-MORROW stare,
   A Muezzín from the Tower of Darkness cries,
"Fools! your Reward is neither Here nor There!"

QUATRAIN XLII

And lately, by the Tavern Door agape,
Came stealing through the Dusk an Angel Shape
   Bearing a Vessel on his Shoulder; and
He bid me taste of it; and 'twas—the Grape!

7

Illustrations

FOLLOWING PAGE 96

QUATRAIN LXXII

Alas, that Spring should vanish with the Rose!
That Youth's sweet-scented Manuscript should close!
　The Nightingale that in the Branches sang,
Ah, whence, and whither flown again, who knows!

The Second Edition of the Translation

QUATRAIN XI

With me along the Strip of Herbage strown
That just divides the desert from the sown,
　Where name of Slave and Sultán is forgot—
And Peace to Máhmúd on his golden Throne?

QUATRAIN XX

The Palace that.to Heav'n his pillars threw,
And Kings the forehead on his threshold drew—
　I saw the solitary Ringdove there,
And "Coo, coo, coo," she cried; and "Coo, coo, coo."

QUATRAIN XLIV

Do you, within your little hour of Grace,
The waving Cypress in your Arms enlace,
　Before the Mother back into her arms
Fold, and dissolve you in a last embrace.

Illustrations

FOLLOWING PAGE 144

QUATRAIN LXXII

Heav'n but the Vision of fulfill'd Desire,
And Hell the Shadow of a Soul on fire,
    Cast on the Darkness into which Ourselves,
So late emerged from, shall so soon expire.

The Fifth Edition of the Translation

QUATRAIN XIV

Look to the blowing Rose about us—"Lo,
Laughing," she says, "into the world I blow,
    At once the silken tassel of my Purse
Tear, and its Treasure on the Garden throw."

QUATRAIN XXXVII

For I remember stopping by the way
To watch a Potter thumping his wet Clay:
    And with its all-obliterated Tongue
It murmur'd—"Gently, Brother, gently, pray!"

QUATRAIN XLI

Perplext no more with Human or Divine,
To-morrow's tangle to the winds resign,
    And lose your fingers in the tresses of
The Cypress-slender Minister of Wine.

9

*E*DWARD FITZGERALD, whom the world has already learned, in spite of his own efforts to remain within the shadow of anonymity, to look upon as one of the rarest poets of the last century, was born at Bredfield, in Suffolk, on the 31st March, 1809. He was the third son of John Purcell, of Kilkenny, in Ireland, who, marrying Miss Mary Frances Fitzgerald, daughter of John Fitzgerald, of Williamstown, County Waterford, added that distinguished name to his own patronymic; and the future Omar was thus doubly of Irish extraction. (Both the families of Purcell and Fitzgerald claim descent from Norman warriors of the eleventh century.) This circumstance is thought to have had some influence in attracting him to the study of Persian poetry, Iran and Erin being almost convertible terms in the early days of modern ethnology. After some years of primary education at the grammar school of

Bury St. Edmunds, he entered Trinity College, Cambridge, in 1826, and there formed acquaintance with several young men of great abilities, most of whom rose to distinction before him, but never ceased to regard with affectionate remembrance the quiet and amiable associate of their college-days. Amongst them were Alfred Tennyson, James Spedding, William Bodham Donne, John Mitchell Kemble, and William Makepeace Thackeray; and their long friendship was touchingly referred to by Tennyson in dedicating his last poem to the memory of Edward Fitzgerald. "Euphranor," our author's earliest printed work, affords a curious picture of his academic life and associations. Its substantial reality is evident beneath the thin disguise of the symbolical or classical names which he gives to the personages of the colloquy; and the speeches which he puts into his own mouth are full of the humorous gravity, and whimsical and kindly philosophy, which remained his distinguishing characteristics till the end. This book was first published in 1851; a second and a third edition were printed some years later; all anonymous, and each of the latter two differing from its predecessor by changes in the text which were not indicated on the title-pages.

"Euphranor" furnishes a good many characterizations which would be useful for any writer treating upon Cambridge society in the third decade of this century. Kenelm Digby, the author of the "Broadstone of Honour," had left Cambridge before the time when Euphranor held his "dialogue," but he is picturesquely recollected as "a grand swarthy fellow who might have stepped out of the canvas of some knightly portrait in his father's hall—perhaps the living image of one sleeping under some cross-legged *effigies* in the church." In "Euphranor," it is easy to discover the earliest phase of the unconquerable attachment which Fitzgerald entertained for his college and his life-long friends, and which induced him in later days to make frequent visits to Cambridge, renewing and refreshing the old ties of custom and friendship. In fact, his disposition was affectionate to a fault, and he betrayed his consciousness of weakness in that respect by referring playfully at times to "a certain natural lubricity" which he attributed to the Irish character, and professed to discover especially in himself. This amiability of temper endeared him to many friends of totally dissimilar tastes and qualities; and, by enlarging his sympathies, enabled him to enjoy the fructifying influence of studies pursued in communion with scholars more profound than himself, but less gifted with the power of expression. One of the younger Cambridge men with whom he became intimate during his periodical pilgrimages to the university, was Edward B. Cowell, a man of the highest attainment in Oriental learning, who resembled Fitzgerald himself in the possession of a warm and genial heart and the most unobtrusive modesty. From Cowell he could easily learn that the hypothetical affinity between the names of Erin and Iran belong to an obsolete stage of etymology; but the attraction of a far-fetched theory was replaced by the charm of reading Persian poetry in companionship with his young friend, who was equally competent to enjoy and to analyze the beauties of a literature that formed a portion of his regular studies. They read together the poetical remains of Khayyám—a choice of reading which sufficiently indicates the depth and range of Mr. Cowell's knowledge. Omar Khayyám, although not quite forgotten, enjoyed in the history of Persian literature a celebrity like that of Occleve and Gower in our own. In the many *Tazkirát* (memoirs or memorials) of Poets, he was mentioned and quoted with esteem; but his poems, laboring as they did under the original sin of heresy and atheism, were seldom looked at, and, from lack of demand on the part of readers, had become rarer than those of most other writers since the days of Firdausi. European scholars knew little of his works beyond his Arabic treatise on Algebra, and Mr. Cowell may be said to have disentombed his poems from oblivion. Now, thanks to the fine taste of that scholar, and to the transmuting genius of Fitzgerald, no Persian poet is so well known in the western world as Abu-'l-fat'h 'Omar, son of Ibrahim the tentmaker of Naishápúr, whose manhood synchronizes with the Norman conquest of England, and who took for his poetic name (*takhallus*) the designation of his father's trade (*Khayyám*). The "Rubá'iyyát" (Quatrains) do not compose a single poem divided into a certain number of stanzas; there is no continuity of plan in them, and each stanza is a distinct thought expressed in musical verse. There is no other element of unity in them than the general tendency of the Epicurean idea, and the arbitrary divan form by which they are grouped according to the alphabetical arrangement of the final letters; those in which the rhymes end in *a* constituting the first division, those with *b* the second, and so on. The peculiar attitude towards religion and the old questions of fate, immortality, the origin and the destiny of man, which educated thinkers have assumed in the present age of Christendom, is found admirably foreshadowed in the fantastic verses of Khayyám, who was no more of a Mohammedan than many of our best writers are Christians. His philosophical and Horatian fancies—graced as they are by the charms of a lyrical expression equal to that of Horace, and a vivid brilliance of imagination to which the Roman poet could make no claim—exercised a powerful influence upon Fitzgerald's mind, and colored his thoughts to such a degree that even when he oversteps the largest license allowed to a translator, his phrases reproduce the spirit and manner of his original with a nearer approach to perfection than would appear possible. It is usually supposed that there is more of Fitzgerald than of Khayyám in the English "Rubá'iyyát," and that the old Persian simply afforded themes for the Anglo-Irishman's display of poetic power; but nothing could be further from the truth. The French translator, J. B. Nicolas, and the English one, Mr. Whinfield, supply a closer mechanical reflection of the sense in each separate stanza; but Mr. Fitzgerald has, in some instances, given a version equally close and exact; in others, rejointed scattered phrases from more than one stanza of his original, and thus accomplished a feat of marvelous poetical transfusion. He frequently turns literally into English the strange outlandish imagery which Mr. Whinfield thought necessary to replace by more intelligible banalities, and in this way the magic of his genius has successfully transplanted into the garden of English poesy exotics that bloom like native flowers.

One of Mr. Fitzgerald's Woodbridge friends was Bernard Barton, the Quaker poet, with whom he maintained for many years the most intimate and cordial intercourse, and whose daughter Lucy he married. He wrote the memoir of his friend's life which appeared in the posthumous volume of Barton's poems. The story of his married life was a short one. With all the overflowing amiability of his nature, there were mingled certain peculiarities or waywardnesses which were more suitable to the freedom of celibacy than to the staidness of matrimonial life. A separation took place by mutual agreement, and Fitzgerald behaved in this circumstance with the generosity and unselfishness which were apparent in all his whims no less than in his more deliberate actions. Indeed, his entire career was marked by an unchanging goodness of heart and a genial kindliness; and no one could complain of having ever endured hurt or ill-treatment at his hands. His pleasures were innocent and simple. Amongst the more delightful, he counted the short coasting trips, occupying no more than a day or two at a time, which he used to make in his own yacht from Lowestoft, accompanied only by a crew of two men, and such a friend as Cowell, with a large pasty and a few bottles of wine to supply their material wants. It is needless to say that books were also put into the cabin, and that the symposia of the friends were thus brightened by communion with the minds of the great departed. Fitzgerald's enjoyment of gnomic wisdom enshrined in words of exquisite propriety was evinced by the frequency with which he used to read Montaigne's essays and Madame de Sévigné's letters, and the various works from which he extracted and published his collection of wise saws entitled "Polonius." This taste was allied to a love for what was classical and correct in literature, by which he was also enabled to appreciate the prim and formal muse of Crabbe, in whose grandson's house he died.

His second printed work was the "Polonius," already referred to, which appeared in 1852. It exemplifies his favorite reading, being a collection of extracts, sometimes short proverbial phrases, sometimes longer pieces of characterization or reflection, arranged under abstract headings. He occasionally quotes Dr. Johnson, for whom he entertains sincere admiration; but the ponderous and artificial fabric of Johnsonese did not please him like the language of Bacon, Fuller, Sir Thomas Browne, Coleridge, whom he cites frequently. A disproportionate abundance of wise words was drawn from Carlyle; his original views, his forcible sense, and the friendship with which Fitzgerald regarded him, having apparently blinded the latter to the ungainly style and ungraceful mannerisms of the Chelsea sage. (It was Thackeray who first made them personally acquainted; and Fitzgerald remained always loyal to his first instincts of affection and admiration.) Polonius also marks the period of his earliest attention to Persian studies, as he quotes in it the great Súfi poet, Jalál-ud-dín-Rúmi, whose "Masnavi" has been translated into English by Mr. Redhouse, but whom Fitzgerald can only have seen in the original. He, however, spells the name *Jallaladin,* an incorrect form of which he could not have been guilty at the time when he produced Omar Khayyám, and which thus betrays that he had not long been engaged with Irani literature. He was very fond of Montaigne's essays, and of Pascal's "Pensées"; but his "Polonius" reveals a sort of dislike and contempt for Voltaire. Amongst the Germans, Jean Paul, Goethe, Alexander von Humboldt and August Wilhelm von Schlegel attracted him greatly; but he seems to have read little German, and probably only quoted translations. His favorite motto was "Plain Living and High Thinking," and he expresses great reverence for all things manly, simple, and true. The laws and institutions of England were, in his eyes, of the highest value and sacredness; and whatever Irish sympathies he had would never have diverted his affections from the Union to Home Rule. This is strongly illustrated by some original lines of blank verse at the end of "Polonius," annexed to his quotation, under "Æsthetics," of the words in which Lord Palmerston eulogized Mr. Gladstone for having devoted his Neopolitan tour to an inspection of the prisons.

Fitzgerald's next printed work was a translation of Six Dramas of Calderón, published in 1853, which was unfavorably received at the time, and consequently withdrawn by him from circulation. His name appeared on the title-page, —a concession to publicity which was so unusual with him that it must have been made under strong pressure from his friends. The book is in nervous blank verse, a mode of composition which he handled with great ease and skill. There is no waste of power in diffuseness and no employment of unnecessary epithets. It gives the impression of a work of the Shakespearean age, and reveals a kindred felicity, strength, and directness of language. It deserves to rank with his best efforts in poetry, but its ill-success made him feel that the publication of his name was an unfavorable experiment, and he never again repeated it. His great modesty, however, would sufficiently account for his shyness. Of "Omar Khay-yám," even after the little book had won its way to general esteem, he used to say that the suggested addition of his name on the title would imply an assumption of importance which he considered that his "transmogrification" of the Persian poet did not possess.

Fitzgerald's conception of a translator's privilege is well set forth in the prefaces of his versions from Calderón, and the "Agamemnon" of Æschylus. He maintained that, in the absence of the perfect poet, who shall re-create in his own language the body and soul of his original, the best system is that of a paraphrase conserving the spirit of the author,—a sort of literary metempsychosis. Calderón, Æschylus, and Omar Khayyám were all treated with equal license, so far as form is concerned,—the last, perhaps, the most arbitrarily; but the result is not unsatisfactory as having given us perfect English poems instinct with the true flavor of their proto-types. The Persian was probably somewhat more Horatian and less melancholy, the Greek a little less florid and mystic, the Spaniard more lyrical and fluent, than their metaphrast has made them; but the essential spirit has not escaped in transfusion. Only a man of singular gifts could have per-

formed the achievement, and these works attest Mr. Fitzgerald's right to rank amongst the finest poets of the century.
About the same time as he printed his Calderón, another set
of translations from the same dramatist was published by the
late D. F. MacCarthy, a scholar whose acquaintance with
Castilian literature was much deeper than Mr. Fitzgerald's,
and who also possessed poetical abilities of no mean order,
with a totally different sense of the translator's duty. The
popularity of MacCarthy's versions has been considerable,
and as an equivalent rendering of the original in sense and
form his work is valuable. Spaniards familiar with the English
language rate its merit highly; but there can be little question
of the very great superiority of Mr. Fitzgerald's work as a
contribution to English literature. It is indeed only from this
point of view that we should regard all the literary labors of
our author. They are English poetical work of fine quality,
dashed with a pleasant outlandish flavor which heightens
their charm; and it is as English poems, not as translations,
that they have endeared themselves even more to the American English than to the mixed Britons of England.

It was an occasion of no small moment to Mr. Fitzgerald's
fame, and to the intellectual gratification of many thousands
of readers, when he took his little packet of "Rubá'iyyát" to
Mr. Quaritch in the latter part of the year 1858. It was
printed as a small quarto pamphlet, bearing the publisher's
name but not the author's; and although apparently a complete failure at first,—a failure which Mr. Fitzgerald regretted
less on his own account than on that of his publisher, to whom

he had generously made a present of the book,—received, nevertheless, a sufficient distribution by being quickly reduced from the price of five shillings and placed in the box of cheap books marked a penny each. Thus forced into circulation, the two hundred copies which had been printed were soon exhausted. Among the buyers were Dante Gabriel Rossetti, Swinburne, Sir Richard Burton, and William Simpson, the accomplished artist of the *Illustrated London News*. The influence exercised by the first three, especially by Rossetti, upon a clique of young men who later grew to distinction, was sufficient to attract observation to the singular beauties of the poem anonymously translated from the Persian. Most readers had no possible opportunity of discovering whether it was a disguised original or an actual translation;—even Burton enjoyed probably but little chance of seeing a manuscript of the Persian "Rubá'iyyát." The Oriental imagery and allusions were too thickly scattered throughout the verses to favor the notion that they could be the original work of an Englishman; yet it was shrewdly suspected by most of the appreciative readers that the "translator" was substantially the author and creator of the poem. In the refuge of his anonymity, Fitzgerald derived an innocent gratification from the curiosity that was aroused on all sides. After the first edition had disappeared, inquiries for the little book became frequent, and in the year 1868 he gave the MS. of his second edition to Mr. Quaritch, and the "Rubá'iyyát" came into circulation once more, but with several alterations and additions by which the number of stanzas was somewhat increased beyond the original seventy-five. Most of the changes were, as might have been expected, improvements; but in some instances the author's taste or caprice was at fault,—notably in the first *Rubá'iy*. His fastidious desire to avoid anything that seemed *baroque* or unnatural or appeared like plagiarism, may have influenced him; but it was probably because he had already used the idea in his rendering of Jámí's "Salámán," that he sacrificed a fine and novel piece of imagery in his first stanza and replaced it by one of much more ordinary character. If it were from a dislike to pervert his original too largely, he had no need to be so scrupulous, since he dealt on the whole with the "Rubá'iyyát" as though he had the license of absolute authorship, changing, transposing, and manipulating the substance of the Persian quatrains with a singular freedom. The vogue of "old Omar" (as he would affectionately call his work) went on increasing, and American readers took it up with eagerness. In those days the mere mention of Omar Khayyám between two strangers meeting fortuitously acted like a sign of freemasonry and established frequently a bond of friendship. Some curious instances of this have been related. A remarkable feature of the Omar-cult in the United States was the circumstance that single individuals bought numbers of copies for gratuitous distribution before the book was reprinted in America. Its editions have been relatively numerous, when we consider how restricted was the circle of readers who could understand the peculiar beauties of the work. A third edition appeared in 1872, with some further alterations, and may be regarded as virtually the author's final revision, for it hardly differs at all from the text of the fourth edition, which appeared in 1879. This last formed the first portion of a volume entitled "Rubáiyát of Omar Khayyám; and the Salámán and Absál of Jámí; rendered into English verse." The "Salámán" (which had already been printed in separate form in 1856) is a poem chiefly in blank verse, interspersed with various meters (although it is all in one measure in the original) embodying a love-story of mystic significance; for Jámí was, unlike Omar Khay-yám, a true Súfi, and indeed differed in other respects, his celebrity as a pious Mussulman doctor being equal to his fame as a poet. He lived in the fifteenth century, in a period of literary brilliance and decay; and the rich exuberance of his poetry, full of far-fetched conceits, involved expressions, overstrained imagery, and false taste, offers a strong contrast to the simpler and more forcible language of Khayyám. There is little use of Arabic in the earlier poet; he preferred the vernacular speech to the mongrel language which was fashionable among the heirs of the Saracen conquerors; but Jámí's composition is largely embroidered with Arabic.

Mr. Fitzgerald had from his early days been thrown into contact with the Crabbe family; the Reverend George Crabbe (the poet's grandson) was an intimate friend of his, and it was on a visit to Morton Rectory that Fitzgerald died. As we know that friendship has power to warp the judgment, we shall not probably be wrong in supposing that his enthusiastic admiration for Crabbe's poems was not the product of sound, impartial criticism. He attempted to reintroduce them to the world by publishing a little volume of "Readings from Crabbe," produced in the last year of his life, but without success. A different fate awaited his "Agamemnon: a tragedy taken from Æschylus," which was first printed privately by him, and afterwards published with alterations in 1876. It is a very free rendering from the Greek, and full of a poetical beauty which is but partly assignable to Æschylus. Without attaining to anything like the celebrity and admiration which have followed Omar Khayyám, the "Agamemnon" has achieved much more than a *succès d'estime*. Mr. Fitzgerald's renderings from the Greek were not confined to this one essay; he also translated the two Œdipus dramas of Sopho-cles, but left them unfinished in manuscript till Prof. Eliot Norton had a sight of them and urged him to complete his work. When this was done, he had them set in type, but only a very few proofs can have been struck off, as it seems that, at least in England, no more than one or two copies were sent out by the author. In a similar way he printed transla-tions of two of Calderón's plays not included in the published "Six Dramas"—namely, "La Vida es Sueño," and "El Mágico Prodigioso" (both ranking among the Spaniard's finest work); but they also were withheld from the public and all but half a dozen friends.

When his old boatman died, he abandoned his nautical exercises and gave up his yacht forever. During the last few years of his life, he divided his time between Cambridge, Crabbe's house, and his own home at Little Grange, near Woodbridge, where he received occasional visits from friends and relatives. He was one of the most modest men who have enriched English literature with poetry of distinct and permanent value, and his best epitaph is found in Tennyson's "Tiresias and other Poems," published immediately after our author's quiet exit from life, in 1883, in the seventy-fifth year of his age.

OMAR KHAYYÁM

The Astronomer-Poet of Persia

BY EDWARD FITZGERALD

OMAR KHAYYÁM was born at Naishápúr in Khorassán in the latter half of our Eleventh, and died within the First Quarter of our Twelfth Century. The slender story of his life is curiously twined about that of two other very considerable Figures in their Time and Country: one of whom tells the Story of all Three. This was Nizám ul Mulk, Vizyr to Alp Arslan the Son, and Malik Shah the Grandson, of Toghrul Beg the Tartar, who had wrested Persia from the feeble Successor of Mahmúd the Great, and founded that Seljukian Dynasty which finally roused Europe into the Crusades. This Nizám ul Mulk, in his *Wasiyat*—or *Testament*—which he wrote and left as a Memorial for future Statesmen—relates the following, as quoted in the *Calcutta Review*, No. 59, from Mirkhond's History of the Assassins

"One of the greatest of the wise men of Khorassán was the

2 7

Imám Mowaffak of Naishápúr, a man highly honored and reverenced,—may God rejoice his soul: his illustrious years exceeded eighty-five, and it was the universal belief that every boy who read the Koran or studied the traditions in his presence, would assuredly attain to honor and happiness. For this cause did my father send me from Tús to Naishápúr with Abd-us-samad, the doctor of law, that I might employ myself in study and learning under the guidance of that illustrious teacher. Towards me he ever turned an eye of favor and kindness, and as his pupil I felt for him extreme affection and devotion, so that I passed four years in his service. When I first came there, I found two other pupils of mine own age newly arrived, Hakim Omar Khayyám, and the ill-fated Ben Sabbáh. Both were endowed with sharpness of wit and the highest natural powers; and we three formed a close friend-ship together. When the Imám rose from his lectures, they used to join me, and we repeated to each other the lessons we had heard. Now Omar was a native of Naishápúr, while Hasan Ben Sabbáh's father was one Ali, a man of austere life and practice, but heretical in his creed and doctrine. One day Hasan said to me and to Khayyám, 'It is a universal belief that the pupils of the Imám Mowaffak will attain to fortune. Now, even if we *all* do not attain thereto, without doubt one of us will; what then shall be our mutual pledge and bond?' We answered, 'Be it what you please.' 'Well,' he said, 'let us make a vow, that to whomsoever this fortune falls, he shall share it equally with the rest, and reserve no pre-eminence for himself.' 'Be it so,' we both replied, and on those terms we mutually pledged our words. Years rolled on, and I went from Khorassán to Transoxiana and wandered to Ghazni and Cabul; and when I returned, I was invested with office, and rose to be administrator of affairs during the Sultanate of Sultan Alp Arslan.

"He goes on to state, that years passed by, and both his old school-friends found him out, and came and claimed a share in his good fortune, according to the school-day vow. The Vizier was generous and kept his word. Hasan demanded a place in the government, which the Sultan granted at the Vizier's request; but discontented with a gradual rise, he plunged into the maze of intrigue of an oriental court, and, failing in a base attempt to supplant his benefactor, he was disgraced and fell. After many mishaps and wanderings, Hasan became the head of the Persian sect of the *Ismailians*, —a party of fanatics who had long murmured in obscurity, but rose to an evil eminence under the guidance of his strong and evil will. In A.D. 1090, he seized the castle of Alamút, in the province of Rúdbar, which lies in the mountainous tract south of the Caspian Sea; and it was from this mountain home he obtained that evil celebrity among the Crusaders as the OLD MAN OF THE MOUNTAINS, and spread terror through the Mohammedan world; and it is yet disputed whether the word *Assassin*, which they have left in the language of modern Europe as their dark memorial, is derived from the *hashish*, or opiate of hemp-leaves (the Indian *bhang*), with which they maddened themselves to the sullen pitch of oriental desperation, or from the name of the founder of the dynasty, whom we have seen in his quiet collegiate days, at Naishápúr. One of the countless victims of the Assassin's dagger was Nizám-ul-Mulk himself, the old schoolboy friend.

"Omar Khayyám also came to the Vizier to claim his share; but not to ask for title or office. 'The greatest boon you can confer on me,' he said, 'is to let me live in a corner under the shadow of your fortune, to spread wide the advantages of Science, and pray for your long life and prosperity.' The Vizier tells us, that when he found Omar was really sincere in his refusal, he pressed him no further, but granted him a yearly pension of 1200 *mithkáls* of gold from the treasury of Naishápúr.

"At Naishápúr thus lived and died Omar Khayyám, 'busied,' adds the Vizier, 'in winning knowledge of every kind, and especially in Astronomy, wherein he attained to a very high pre-eminence. Under the Sultanate of Malik Shah, he came to Merv, and obtained great praise for his proficiency in science, and the Sultan showered favors upon him.'

"When the Malik Shah determined to reform the calendar, Omar was one of the eight learned men employed to do it; the result was the *Jaláli* era (so called from *Jalál-ud-din,* one of the King's names)—'a computation of time,' says Gibbon, 'which surpasses the Julian, and approaches the accuracy of the Gregorian style.' He is also the author of some astronomical tables, entitled Zíji-Maliksháhí, and the French have lately republished and translated an Arabic Treatise of his on Algebra.

"His Takhallus or poetical name (Khayyám) signifies a

Tent-maker, and he is said to have at one time exercised that trade, perhaps before Nizám-ul-Mulk's generosity raised him to independence. Many Persian poets similarly derive their names from their occupations; thus we have Attár, 'a druggist,' Assár, 'an oil presser,' etc. Omar himself alludes to his name in the following whimsical lines:—

" 'Khayyám, who stitched the tents of science,
    Has fallen in grief's furnace and been suddenly burned;
    The shears of Fate have cut the tent ropes of his life,
    And the broker of Hope has sold him for nothing!'

"We have only one more anecdote to give of his Life, and that relates to the close; it is told in the anonymous preface which is sometimes prefixed to his poems; it has been printed in the Persian in the Appendix to Hyde's *Veterum Persarum Religio*, p. 449; and D'Herbelot alludes to it in his Bibliothèque, under *Khiam*,—

"It is written in the chronicles of the ancients that this King of the Wise, Omar Khayyám, died at Naishápúr in the year of the Hegira, 517 (A.D. 1123); in science he was unrivaled,—the very paragon of his age. Khwájah Nizámi of Samarcand, who was one of his pupils, relates the following story: 'I often used to hold conversations with my teacher, Omar Khayyám, in a garden; and one day he said to me, "My tomb shall be in a spot where the north wind may scatter roses over it." I wondered at the words he spake, but I knew that his were no idle words. Years after, when I chanced to revisit Naishápúr, I went to his final resting-place, and lo! it was just outside a garden, and trees laden with fruit stretched their boughs over the garden wall, and dropped their flowers upon his tomb, so that the stone was hidden under them.' "

Thus far—without fear of Trespass—from the *Calcutta Review*. The writer of it, on reading in India this story of Omar's Grave, was reminded, he says, of Cicero's account of finding Archimedes' Tomb at Syracuse, buried in grass and weeds. I think Thorwaldsen desired to have roses grow over him; a wish religiously fulfilled for him to the present day, I believe. However, to return to Omar.

Though the Sultan "shower'd Favors upon him," Omar's Epicurean Audacity of Thought and Speech caused him to be regarded askance in his own Time and Country. He is said to have been especially hated and dreaded by the Súfis, whose Practise he ridiculed, and whose Faith amounts to little more than his own, when stript of the Mysticism and formal recognition of Islamism under which Omar would not hide. Their Poets, including Háfiz, who are (with the exception of Firdausi) the most considerable in Persia, borrowed largely, indeed, of Omar's material, but turning it to a mystical Use more convenient to Themselves and the People they addressed; a People quite as quick of Doubt as of Belief; as keen of Bodily Sense as of Intellectual; and delighting in a cloudy composition of both, in which they could float luxuriously between Heaven and Earth, and this World and the next, on the wings of a poetical expression, that might serve indifferently for either. Omar was too honest of Heart as well of

Head for this. Having failed (however mistakenly) of finding any Providence but Destiny, and any World but This, he set about making the most of it; preferring rather to soothe the Soul through the Senses into Acquiescence with Things as he saw them, than to perplex it with vain disquietude after what they *might* be. It has been seen, however, that his Worldly Ambition was not exorbitant; and he very likely takes a humorous or perverse pleasure in exalting the gratification of Sense above that of the Intellect, in which he must have taken great delight, although it failed to answer the Questions in which he, in common with all men, was most vitally interested.

For whatever Reason, however, Omar, as before said, has never been popular in his own Country, and therefore has been but scantily transmitted abroad. The MSS. of his Poems, mutilated beyond the average Casualties of Oriental Transcription, are so rare in the East as scarce to have reached Westward at all, in spite of all the acquisitions of Arms and Science. There is no copy at the India House, none at the Bibliothèque Nationale of Paris. We know but one in England: No. 140 of the Ouseley MSS. at the Bodleian, written at Shiráz, A.D. 1460. This contains but 158 Rubáiyát. One in the Asiatic Society's Library at Calcutta (of which we have a copy) contains (and yet incomplete) 516, though swelled to that by all kinds of Repetition and Corruption. So Von Hammer speaks of *his* Copy as containing about 200, while Dr. Sprenger catalogues the Lucknow MSS. at double that number. The Scribes, too, of the Oxford and Calcutta MSS.

seem to do their Work under a sort of Protest; each beginning
with a Tetrastich (whether genuine or not) taken out of its
alphabetical order; the Oxford with one of Apology; the Calcutta with one of Expostulation, supposed (says a Notice
prefixed to the MS.) to have arisen from a Dream, in which
Omar's mother asked about his future fate. It may be rendered thus:—

> "Oh Thou who burn'st in Heart for those who burn
> In Hell, whose fires thyself shall feed in turn;
> How long be crying, 'Mercy on them, God!'
> Why, who art Thou to teach, and He to learn?"

The Bodleian Quatrain pleads Pantheism by way of Jus-
tification.

> "If I myself upon a looser Creed
> Have loosely strung the Jewel of Good deed,
> Let this one thing for my Atonement plead:
> That One for Two I never did misread."

The Reviewer to whom I owe the Particulars of Omar's
Life concludes his Review by comparing him with Lucretius,
both as to natural Temper and Genius, and as acted upon
by the Circumstances in which he lived. Both indeed were
men of subtle, strong, and cultivated Intellect, fine Imagination, and Hearts passionate for Truth and Justice; who justly
revolted from their Country's false Religion, and false, or
foolish, Devotion to it; but who fell short of replacing what

they subverted by such better *Hope* as others, with no better Revelation to guide them, had yet made a Law to themselves. Lucretius indeed, with such material as Epicurus furnished, satisfied himself with the theory of a vast machine fortuitously constructed and acting by a Law that implied no Legislator; and so composing himself into a Stoical rather than Epicurean severity of Attitude, sat down to contemplate the mechanical Drama of the Universe which he was part Actor in; himself and all about him (as in his own sublime description of the Roman Theatre) discolored with the lurid reflex of the Curtain suspended between the Spectator and the Sun. Omar, more desperate, or more careless of any so complicated System as resulted in nothing but hopeless Necessity, flung his own Genius and Learning with a bitter or humorous jest into the general Ruin which their insufficient glimpses only served to reveal; and, pretending sensual pleasure, as the serious purpose of Life, only *diverted* himself with speculative problems of Deity, Destiny, Matter and Spirit, Good and Evil, and other such questions, easier to start than to run down, and the pursuit of which becomes a very weary sport at last!

With regard to the present Translation. The original Rubáiyát (as, missing an Arabic Guttural, these *Tetrastichs* are more musically called) are independent Stanzas, consisting each of four Lines of equal though varied Prosody; sometimes *all* rhyming, but oftener (as here imitated) the third line a blank. Somewhat as in the Greek Alcaic, where the penultimate line seems to lift and suspend the Wave that falls over in the last. As usual with such kind of Oriental

Verse, the Rubáiyát follow one another according to Alpha-betic Rhyme—a strange succession of Grave and Gay. Those here selected are strung into something of an Eclogue, with perhaps a less than equal proportion of the "Drink and make-merry," which (genuine or not) recurs over-frequently in the Original. Either way, the Result is sad enough: saddest perhaps when most ostentatiously merry: more apt to move Sorrow than Anger toward the old Tent-maker, who, after vainly endeavoring to unshackle his Steps from Destiny, and to catch some authentic Glimpse of To-morrow, fell back upon To-day (which has outlasted so many To-morrows!) as the only ground he had got to stand upon, however mo-mentarily slipping from under his feet.

While the second Edition of this version of Omar was pre-paring, Monsieur Nicolas, French Consul at Resht, published a very careful and very good Edition of the Text from a lithograph copy at Teheran, comprising 464 Rubáiyát, with translation and notes of his own.

Mons. Nicolas, whose Edition has reminded me of several things, and instructed me in others, does not consider Omar to be the material Epicurean that I have literally taken him for, but a Mystic, shadowing the Deity under the figure of Wine, Wine-bearer, etc., as Háfiz is supposed to do; in short, a Súfi Poet like Háfiz and the rest.

I cannot see reason to alter my opinion, formed as it was more than a dozen years ago when Omar was first shown me by one to whom I am indebted for all I know of Oriental, and very much of other, literature. He admired Omar's genius so much that he would gladly have adopted any such interpretation of his meaning as Mons. Nicolas' if he could. That he could not, appears by his Paper in the *Calcutta Review* already so largely quoted; in which he argues from the Poems themselves, as well as from what records remain of the Poet's Life.

And if more were needed to disprove Mons. Nicolas' Theory, there is the Biographical Notice which he himself has drawn up in direct contradiction to the Interpretation of the Poems given in his Notes. (See pp. xiii–xiv of his Preface.) Indeed I hardly knew poor Omar was so far gone till his Apologist informed me. For here we see that, whatever were the Wine that Háfiz drank and sang, the veritable Juice of the Grape it was which Omar used, not only when carousing with his friends, but (says Mons. Nicolas) in order to excite himself to that pitch of Devotion which others reached by cries and "Hurlemens." And yet, whenever Wine, Wine-bearer, etc., occur in the text—which is often enough—Mons. Nicolas carefully annotates "Dieu," "La Divinité," etc.: so carefully indeed that one is tempted to think that he was indoctrinated by the Súfi with whom he read the Poems. A Persian would naturally wish to vindicate a distinguished Countryman; and a Súfi to enrol him in his own sect, which already comprises all the chief Poets of Persia.

What historical Authority has Mons. Nicolas to show that Omar gave himself up "avec passion à l'étude de la philosophie des Soufis?" (Preface, p. xiii.) The Doctrines of Pantheism, Materialism, Necessity, etc., were not peculiar to the Súfi; nor to Lucretius before them; nor to Epicurus before him; probably the very original Irreligion of Thinking men from the first; and very likely to be the spontaneous growth of a Philosopher living in an Age of social and political barbarism, under shadow of one of the Two and Seventy Religions supposed to divide the world. Von Hammer (according to Sprenger's Oriental Catalogue) speaks of Omar as "a Freethinker, and *a great opponent of sufism;*" perhaps because, while holding much of their Doctrine, he would not pretend to any inconsistent severity of morals. Sir W. Ouseley has written a note to something of the same effect on the fly-leaf of the Bodleian MS. And in two Rubáiyát of Mons. Nicolas' own Edition Súf and Súfi are both disparagingly named.

No doubt many of these Quatrains seem unaccountable unless mystically interpreted; but many more as unaccountable unless literally. Were the Wine spiritual, for instance, how wash the Body with it when dead! Why make cups of the dead clay to be filled with—"La Divinité"—by some succeeding Mystic? Mons. Nicolas himself is puzzled by some "bizarres and trop Orientals" allusions and images—"d'une sensualité quelquefois révoltante" indeed—which "les convenances" do not permit him to translate, but still which the reader cannot but refer to "La Divinité." No doubt also many of the Quatrains in the Teheran, as in the Calcutta Copies, are spurious; such *Rubáiyát* being the common form of Epigram in Persia. But this, at best, tells as much one way as another; nay, the Súfi, who may be considered the Scholar and Men of Letters in Persia, would be far more likely than the careless Epicure to interpolate what favors his own view of the Poet. I observe that very few of the more mystical Quatrains are in the Bodleian MS. which must be one of the oldest, as dated at Shiraz, A.H. 865, A.D. 1460. And this, I think, especially distinguishes Omar (I cannot help calling him by his—no, not Christian—familiar name) from all other Persian Poets: That, whereas with them the Poet is lost in his Song, the Man in Allegory and Abstraction; we seem to have the Man—the *Bonhomme*—Omar himself, with all his Humors and Passions, as frankly before us as if we were really at Table with him, after the Wine had gone round.

I must say that I, for one, never wholly believed in the mysticism of Háfiz. It does not appear there was any danger in holding and singing Súfi Pantheism, so long as the Poet made his Salaam to Mohammed at the beginning and end of his Song. Under such conditions Jeláluddín, Jámí, Attár, and others sang; using Wine and Beauty indeed as Images to illustrate, not as a Mask to hide, the Divinity they were celebrating. Perhaps some Allegory less liable to mistake or abuse had been better among so inflammable a People: much more so when, as some think with Háfiz and Omar, the abstract is not only likened to, but identified with, the sensual Image; hazardous, if not to the Devotee himself, yet to his weaker Brethren; and worse for the Profane in proportion as the Devotion of the Initiated grew warmer. And all for what? To be tantalized with Images of sensual enjoyment which must be renounced if one would approximate a God, who, according to the Doctrine, *is* Sensual Matter as well as Spirit, and into whose Universe one expects unconsciously to merge after Death, without hope of any posthumous Beatitude in another world to compensate for all one's self-denial in this. Lucretius' blind Divinity certainly merited, and probably got, as much self-sacrifice as this of the Súfi; and the burden of Omar's Song—if not "Let us eat"—is assuredly—"Let us drink, for To-morrow we die!" And if Háfiz meant quite otherwise by a similar language, he surely miscalculated when he devoted his Life and Genius to so equivocal a Psalmody as, from his Day to this, has been said and sung by any rather than Spiritual Worshipers.

However, as there is some traditional presumption, and certainly the opinion of some learned men, in favor of Omar's being a Súfi—and even something of a Saint—those who please may so interpret his Wine and Cup-bearer. On the other hand, as there is far more historical certainty of his being a Philosopher, of scientific Insight and Ability far beyond that of the Age and Country he lived in; of such moderate worldly Ambition as becomes a Philosopher, and such moderate wants as rarely satisfy a Debauchee; other readers may be content to believe with me that, while the Wine Omar celebrates is simply the Juice of the Grape, he bragged more than he drank of it, in very defiance perhaps of that Spiritual Wine which left its Votaries sunk in Hypocrisy or Disgust.

I

AWAKE! for Morning in the Bowl of Night
Has flung the Stone that puts the Stars to Flight:
  And Lo! the Hunter of the East has caught
The Sultán's Turret in a Noose of Light.

II

Dreaming when Dawn's Left Hand was in the Sky
I heard a Voice within the Tavern cry,
   "Awake, my Little ones, and fill the Cup
Before Life's Liquor in its Cup be dry."

III

And, as the Cock crew, those who stood before
The Tavern shouted—"Open then the Door!
   You know how little while we have to stay,
And, once departed, may return no more."

IV

Now the New Year reviving old Desires,
The thoughtful Soul to Solitude retires,
 Where the WHITE HAND OF MOSES on the Bough
Puts out, and Jesus from the Ground suspires.

V

Irám indeed is gone with all its Rose,
And Jamshýd's Sev'n-ring'd Cup where no one knows;
 But still the Vine her ancient Ruby yields,
And still a Garden by the Water blows.

VI

And David's Lips are lock't; but in divine
High piping Pehleví, with "Wine! Wine! Wine!
    Red Wine!"—the Nightingale cries to the Rose
That yellow Cheek of hers to incarnadine.

VII

Come, fill the Cup, and in the Fire of Spring
The Winter Garment of Repentance fling:
    The Bird of Time has but a little way
To fly—and Lo! the Bird is on the Wing.

VIII

And look—a thousand Blossoms with the Day
Woke—and a thousand scatter'd into Clay:
   And this first Summer Month that brings the Rose
Shall take Jamshýd and Kaikobád away.

IX

But come with old Khayyám, and leave the Lot
Of Kaikobád and Kaikhosrú forgot:
   Let Rustum lay about him as he will,
Or Hátim Tai cry Supper—heed them not.

X

With me along some Strip of Herbage strown
That just divides the desert from the sown,
    Where name of Slave and Sultán scarce is known,
And pity Sultán Máhmúd on his Throne.

XI

Here with a Loaf of Bread beneath the Bough,
A Flask of Wine, a Book of Verse—and Thou
    Beside me singing in the Wilderness—
And Wilderness is Paradise enow.

XII

"How sweet is mortal Sovranty!"—think some:
Others—"How blest the Paradise to come!"
    Ah, take the Cash in hand and waive the Rest;
Oh, the brave Music of a *distant* Drum!

XIII

Look to the Rose that blows about us—"Lo,
Laughing," she says, "into the World I blow:
    At once the silken Tassel of my Purse
Tear, and its Treasure on the Garden throw."

XIV

The Worldly Hope men set their Hearts upon
Turns Ashes—or it prospers; and anon,
   Like Snow upon the Desert's dusty Face
Lighting a little Hour or two—is gone.

XV

And those who husbanded the Golden Grain,
And those who flung it to the Winds like Rain,
   Alike to no such aureate Earth are turn'd
As, buried once, Men want dug up again.

QUATRAIN I   p. 41

[First Edition of the Translation]

Awake! for Morning in the Bowl of Night
Has flung the Stone that puts the Stars to Flight:
　And Lo! the Hunter of the East has caught
The Sultán's Turret in a Noose of Light.

QUATRAIN XI p. 46

[*First Edition of the Translation*]

Here with a Loaf of Bread beneath the Bough,
A Flask of Wine, a Book of Verse—and Thou
  Beside me singing in the Wilderness—
And Wilderness is Paradise enow.

QUATRAIN XXIV p. 53

[*First Edition of the Translation*]

Alike for those who for TO-DAY prepare,
And those that after a TO-MORROW stare,
  A Muezzín from the Tower of Darkness cries,
"Fools! your Reward is neither Here nor There!"

QUATRAIN XLII   p. 62

[First Edition of the Translation]

And lately, by the Tavern Door agape,
Came stealing through the Dusk an Angel Shape
    Bearing a Vessel on his Shoulder; and
He bid me taste of it; and 'twas—the Grape!

XVI

Think, in this batter'd Caravanserai
Whose Doorways are alternate Night and Day,
How Sultán after Sultán with his Pomp
Abode his Hour or two, and went his way.

XVII

They say the Lion and the Lizard keep
The Courts where Jamshýd gloried and drank deep;
And Bahrám, that great Hunter—the Wild Ass
Stamps o'er his Head, and he lies fast asleep.

XVIII

I sometimes think that never blows so red
The Rose as where some buried Cæsar bled;
    That every Hyacinth the Garden wears
Dropt in its Lap from some once lovely Head.

XIX

And this delightful Herb whose tender Green
Fledges the River's Lip on which we lean—
    Ah, lean upon it lightly! for who knows
From what once lovely Lip it springs unseen!

XX

Ah, my Belovéd, fill the Cup that clears
To-DAY of past Regrets and future Fears—
　　To-morrow?—Why, To-morrow I may be
Myself with Yesterday's Sev'n Thousand Years.

XXI

Lo! some we loved, the loveliest and the best
That Time and Fate of all their Vintage prest,
　　Have drunk their Cup a Round or two before,
And one by one crept silently to Rest.

XXII

And we, that now make merry in the Room
They left, and Summer dresses in new Bloom,
   Ourselves must we beneath the Couch of Earth
Descend, ourselves to make a Couch—for whom?

XXIII

Ah, make the most of what we yet may spend,
Before we too into the Dust descend;
   Dust into Dust, and under Dust, to lie,
Sans Wine, sans Song, sans Singer, and—sans End.

XXIV

Alike for those who for To-DAY prepare,
And those that after a To-MORROW stare,
   A Muezzín from the Tower of Darkness cries
"Fools! your Reward is neither Here nor There!"

XXV

Why, all the Saints and Sages who discuss'd
Of the Two Worlds so learnedly, are thrust
   Like foolish Prophets forth; their Words to Scorn
Are scatter'd, and their Mouths are stopt with Dust.

XXVI

Oh, come with old Khayyám, and leave the Wise
To talk; one thing is certain, that Life flies;
  One thing is certain, and the Rest is Lies;
The Flower that once has blown for ever dies.

XXVII

Myself when young did eagerly frequent
Doctor and Saint, and heard great Argument
  About it and about: but evermore
Came out by the same Door as in I went.

XXVIII

With them the Seed of Wisdom did I sow,
And with my own hand labour'd it to grow:
   And this was all the Harvest that I reap'd—
"I came like Water, and like Wind I go."

XXIX

Into this Universe, and *why* not knowing,
Nor *whence*, like Water willy-nilly flowing;
   And out of it, as Wind along the Waste,
I know not *whither*, willy-nilly blowing.

XXX

What, without asking, hither hurried *whence?*
And, without asking, *whither* hurried hence!
    Another and another Cup to drown
The Memory of this Impertinence!

XXXI

Up from Earth's Centre through the Seventh Gate
I rose, and on the Throne of Saturn sate,
    And many Knots unravel'd by the Road;
But not the Knot of Human Death and Fate.

XXXII

There was a Door to which I found no Key:
There was a Veil past which I could not see:
  Some little Talk awhile of ME and THEE
There seem'd—and then no more of THEE and ME.

XXXIII

Then to the rolling Heav'n itself I cried,
Asking, "What Lamp had Destiny to guide
  Her little Children stumbling in the Dark?"
And—"A blind Understanding!" Heav'n replied.

XXXIV

Then to this earthen Bowl did I adjourn
My Lip the secret Well of Life to learn:
    And Lip to Lip it murmur'd—"While you live
Drink!—for once dead you never shall return."

XXXV

I think the Vessel, that with fugitive
Articulation answer'd, once did live,
    And merry-make; and the cold Lip I kiss'd
How many Kisses might it take—and give!

XXXVI

For in the Market-place, one Dusk of Day,
I watch'd the Potter thumping his wet Clay:
    And with its all obliterated Tongue
It murmur'd—"Gently, Brother, gently, pray!"

XXXVII

Ah, fill the Cup:—what boots it to repeat
How Time is slipping underneath our Feet:
    Unborn To-morrow, and dead Yesterday
Why fret about them if To-day be sweet!

XXXVIII

One Moment in Annihilation's Waste,
One Moment, of the Well of Life to taste—
　The Stars are setting and the Caravan
Starts for the Dawn of Nothing—Oh, make haste!

XXXIX

How long, how long, in definite Pursuit
Of This and That endeavour and dispute?
　Better be merry with the fruitful Grape
Than sadder after none, or bitter, Fruit.

XL

You know, my Friends, how long since in my House
For a new Marriage I did make Carouse:
   Divorced old barren Reason from my Bed,
And took the Daughter of the Vine to Spouse.

XLI

For "Is" and "Is-NOT" though *with* Rule and Line
And "UP-AND-DOWN" *without,* I could define,
   I yet in all I only cared to know,
Was never deep in anything but—Wine.

XLII

And lately, by the Tavern Door agape,
Came stealing through the Dusk an Angel Shape
   Bearing a Vessel on his Shoulder; and
He bid me taste of it; and 'twas—the Grape!

XLIII

The Grape that can with Logic absolute
The Two-and-Seventy jarring Sects confute:
   The subtle Alchemist that in a Trice
Life's leaden Metal into Gold transmute.

XLIV

The mighty Mahmúd, the victorious Lord,
That all the misbelieving and black Horde
  Of Fears and Sorrows that infest the Soul
Scatters and slays with his enchanted Sword.

XLV

But leave the Wise to wrangle, and with me
The Quarrel of the Universe let be:
  And, in some corner of the Hubbub coucht,
Make Game of that which makes as much of Thee.

XLVI

For in and out, above, about, below,
'Tis nothing but a Magic Shadow-show
   Play'd in a Box whose Candle is the Sun,
Round which we Phantom Figures come and go.

XLVII

And if the Wine you drink, the Lip you press,
End in the Nothing all Things end in—Yes—
   Then fancy while Thou art, Thou art but what
Thou shalt be—Nothing—Thou shalt not be less.

XLVIII

While the Rose blows along the River Brink,
With old Khayyám the Ruby Vintage drink:
    And when the Angel with his darker Draught
Draws up to Thee—take that, and do not shrink.

XLIX

'Tis all a Chequer-board of Nights and Days
Where Destiny with Men for Pieces plays:
    Hither and thither moves, and mates, and slays,
And one by one back in the Closet lays.

L

The Ball no Question makes of Ayes and Noes,
But Right or Left as strikes the Player goes;
    And He that toss'd Thee down into the Field,
He knows about it all—HE knows—HE knows!

LI

The Moving Finger writes; and, having writ,
Moves on: nor all thy Piety nor Wit
    Shall lure it back to cancel half a Line,
Nor all thy Tears wash out a Word of it.

LII

And that inverted Bowl we call The Sky,
Whereunder crawling coop't we live and die,
    Lift not thy hands to *It* for help—for It
Rolls impotently on as Thou or I.

LIII

With Earth's first Clay They did the Last Man's knead,
And then of the Last Harvest sow'd the Seed:
    Yea, the first Morning of Creation wrote
What the Last Dawn of Reckoning shall read.

LIV

I tell Thee this—When, starting from the Goal,
Over the shoulders of the flaming Foal
   Of Heav'n and Parwín and Mushtara they flung,
In my predestined Plot of Dust and Soul.

LV

The Vine had struck a Fibre; which about
If clings my Being—let the Súfi flout;
   Of my Base Metal may be filed a Key,
'That shall unlock the Door he howls without.

LVI

And this I know: whether the one True Light,
Kindle to Love, or Wrath consume me quite,
    One glimpse of It within the Tavern caught
Better than in the Temple lost outright.

LVII

Oh, Thou, who didst with Pitfall and with Gin
Beset the Road I was to wander in,
    Thou wilt not with Predestination round
Enmesh me, and impute my Fall to Sin?

LVIII

Oh, Thou, who Man of baser Earth didst make,
And who with Eden didst devise the Snake;
   For all the Sin wherewith the Face of Man
Is blacken'd, Man's Forgiveness give—and take!

*   *   *   *   *

KÚZA-NÁMA

LIX

Listen again. One evening at the Close
Of Ramazán, ere the better Moon arose,
   In that old Potter's Shop I stood alone
With the clay Population round in Rows.

LX

And, strange to tell, among the Earthen Lot
Some could articulate, while others not:
    And suddenly one more impatient cried—
"Who *is* the Potter, pray, and who the Pot?"

LXI

Then said another—"Surely not in vain
My Substance from the common Earth was ta'en,
    That He who subtly wrought me into Shape
Should stamp me back to common Earth again."

LXII

Another said—"Why, ne'er a peevish Boy,
Would break the Bowl from which he drank in Joy;
   Shall He that *made* the Vessel in pure Love
And Fancy, in an after Rage destroy!"

LXIII

None answer'd this; but after Silence spake
A Vessel of a more ungainly Make:
   "They sneer at me for leaning all awry;
What! did the Hand then of the Potter shake?"

LXIV

Said one—"Folks of a surly Tapster tell,
And daub his Visage with the Smoke of Hell;
   They talk of some strict Testing of us—Pish!
He's a Good Fellow, and 'twill all be well."

LXV

Then said another with a long-drawn Sigh,
"My Clay with long oblivion is gone dry:
   But, fill me with the old familiar Juice,
Methinks I might recover by-and-by!"

LXVI

So while the Vessels one by one were speaking,
One spied the little Crescent all were seeking:
   And then they jogg'd each other, "Brother, Brother!
Hark to the Porter's Shoulder-knot a creaking!"

*   *   *   *   *

LXVII

Ah, with the Grape my fading Life provide,
And wash my Body whence the Life has died,
   And in a Windingsheet of Vine-leaf wrapt,
So bury me by some sweet Garden-side.

LXVIII

That ev'n my buried Ashes such a Snare
Of Perfume shall fling up into the Air,
   As not a True Believer passing by
But shall be overtaken unaware.

LXIX

Indeed the Idols I have loved so long
Have done my Credit in Men's Eye much wrong:
   Have drown'd my Honour in a shallow Cup,
And sold my Reputation for a Song.

LXX

Indeed, indeed, Repentance oft before
I swore—but was I sober when I swore?
  And then and then came Spring, and Rose-in-hand
My thread-bare Penitence apieces tore.

LXXI

And much as Wine has play'd the Infidel,
And robb'd me of my Robe of Honour—well,
  I often wonder what the Vintners buy
One half so precious as the Goods they sell.

LXXII

Alas, that Spring should vanish with the Rose!
That Youth's sweet-scented Manuscript should close!
  The Nightingale that in the Branches sang,
Ah, whence, and whither flown again, who knows!

LXXIII

Ah, Love! could thou and I with Fate conspire
To grasp this sorry Scheme of Things entire,
  Would not we shatter it to bits—and then
Re-mould it nearer to the Heart's Desire!

LXXIV

Ah, Moon of my Delight, who know'st no wane,
The Moon of Heav'n is rising once again:
    How oft hereafter rising shall she look
Through this same Garden after me—in vain!

LXXV

And when Thyself with shining Foot shall pass
Among the Guests Star-scatter'd on the Grass,
    And in thy joyous Errand reach the Spot
Where I made one—turn down an empty Glass!

TAMÁM SHUD

I

WAKE! For the Sun behind yon Eastern height
Has chased the Session of the Stars from Night;
    And, to the field of Heav'n ascending, strikes
The Sultán's Turret with a Shaft of Light.

II

Before the phantom of False morning died,
Methought a Voice within the Tavern cried,
    "When all the Temple is prepared within,
Why lags the drowsy Worshipper outside?"

III

And, as the Cock crew, those who stood before
The Tavern shouted—"Open then the Door!
    You know how little while we have to stay,
And, once departed, may return no more."

IV

Now the New Year reviving old Desires,
The thoughtful Soul to Solitude retires,
    Where the WHITE HAND OF MOSES on the Bough
Puts out, and Jesus from the Ground suspires.

V

Iram indeed is gone with all his Rose,
And Jamshýd's Sev'n-ring'd Cup where no one knows;
    But still a Ruby gushes from the Vine,
And many a Garden by the Water blows.

VI

And David's lips are lockt; but in divine
High-piping Péhleví, with "Wine! Wine! Wine!
    Red Wine!"—the Nightingale cries to the Rose
That sallow cheek of hers to incarnadine.

VII

Come, fill the Cup, and in the fire of Spring
Your Winter-garment of Repentance fling:
    The Bird of Time has but a little way
To flutter—and the Bird is on the Wing.

VIII

Whether at Naishápúr or Babylon,
Whether the Cup with sweet or bitter run,
   The Wine of Life keeps oozing drop by drop,
The Leaves of Life keep falling one by one.

IX

Morning a thousand Roses brings, you say;
Yes, but where leaves the Rose of Yesterday?
   And this first Summer month that brings the Rose
Shall take Jamshýd and Kaikobád away.

X

Well, let it take them! What have we to do
With Kaikobád the Great, or Kaikhosrú?
    Let Rustum cry "To Battle!" as he likes,
Or Hátim Tai "To Supper"—heed not you.

XI

With me along the Strip of Herbage strown
That just divides the desert from the sown,
    Where name of Slave and Sultán is forgot—
And Peace to Máhmúd on his golden Throne?

XII

Here with a little Bread beneath the Bough,
A Flask of Wine, a Book of Verse—and Thou
   Beside me singing in the Wilderness—
Oh, Wilderness were Paradise enow!

XIII

Some for the Glories of This World; and some
Sigh for the Prophet's Paradise to come;
   Ah, take the Cash, and let the promise go,
Nor heed the music of a distant Drum!

XIV

Were it not Folly, Spider-like to spin
The Thread of present Life away to win—
    What? for ourselves, who know not if we shall
Breathe out the very Breath we now breathe in!

XV

Look to the blowing Rose about us—"Lo,
Laughing," she says, "into the world I blow:
    At once the silken tassel of my Purse
Tear, and its Treasure on the Garden throw."

XVI

For those who husbanded the Golden grain,
And those who flung it to the winds like Rain,
   Alike to no such aureate Earth are turn'd
As, buried once, Men want dug up again.

XVII

The Worldly Hope men set their Hearts upon
Turns Ashes—or it prospers; and anon,
   Like Snow upon the Desert's dusty Face,
Lighting a little hour or two—was gone.

XVIII

Think, in this batter'd Caravanserai
Whose Portals are alternate Night and Day,
　How Sultán after Sultán with his Pomp
Abode his destined Hour, and went his way.

XIX

They say the Lion and the Lizard keep
The Courts where Jamshýd gloried and drank deep:
　And Bahrám, that great Hunter—the Wild Ass
Stamps o'er his Head, but cannot break his Sleep.

XX

The Palace that to Heav'n his pillars threw,
And Kings the forehead on his threshold drew—
   I saw the solitary Ringdove there,
And "Coo, coo, coo," she cried; and "Coo, coo, coo."

XXI

Ah, my Belovéd, fill the Cup that clears
To-DAY of past Regret and Future Fears:
   To-morrow!—Why, To-morrow I may be
Myself with Yesterday's Sev'n thousand Years.

XXII

For some we loved, the loveliest and the best
That from his Vintage rolling Time has prest,
   Have drunk their Cup a Round or two before,
And one by one crept silently to rest.

XXIII

And we, that now make merry in the Room
They left, and Summer dresses in new bloom,
Ourselves must we beneath the Couch of Earth
Descend—ourselves to make a Couch—for whom?

XXIV

I sometimes think that never blows so red
The Rose as where some buried Cæsar bled;
   That every Hyacinth the Garden wears
Dropt in her Lap from some once lovely Head.

XXV

And this delightful Herb whose living Green
Fledges the River's Lip on which we lean—
   Ah, lean upon it lightly! for who knows
From what once lovely Lip it springs unseen!

XXVI

Ah, make the most of what we yet may spend,
Before we too into the Dust descend;
   Dust into Dust, and under Dust, to lie,
Sans Wine, sans Song, sans Singer, and—sans End!

XXVII

Alike for those who for To-DAY prepare,
And those that after some To-MORROW stare,
   A Muezzín from the Tower of Darkness cries,
"Fools! your Reward is neither Here nor There."

XXVIII

Another Voice, when I am sleeping, cries,
"The Flower should open with the Morning skies."
   And a retreating Whisper, as I wake—
"The Flower that once has blown for ever dies."

XXIX

Why, all the Saints and Sages who discuss'd
Of the Two Worlds so learnedly, are thrust
   Like foolish Prophets forth; their Words to Scorn
Are scatter'd, and their Mouths are stopt with Dust.

XXX

Myself when young did eagerly frequent
Doctor and Saint, and heard great argument
   About it and about: but evermore
Came out by the same door as in I went.

XXXI

With them the seed of Wisdom did I sow,
And with my own hand wrought to make it grow;
   And this was all the Harvest that I reap'd—
"I came like Water, and like Wind I go."

XXXII

Into this Universe, and *Why* not knowing,
Nor *Whence*, like Water willy-nilly flowing;
   And out of it, as Wind along the Waste,
I know not *Whither*, willy-nilly blowing.

XXXIII

What, without asking, hither hurried *Whence?*
And, without asking, *Whither* hurried hence!
   Ah! contrite Heav'n endowed us with the Vine
To drug the memory of that insolence!

XXXIV

Up from Earth's Centre through the Seventh Gate
I rose, and on the Throne of Saturn sate;
   And many Knots unravel'd by the Road;
But not the Master-Knot of Human Fate.

XXXV

There was the Door to which I found no Key:
There was the Veil through which I could not see:
   Some little talk awhile of ME and THEE
There was—and then no more of THEE and ME.

QUATRAIN LXXII p. 77

[First Edition of the Translation]

Alas, that Spring should vanish with the Rose!
That Youth's sweet-scented Manuscript should close!
The Nightingale that in the Branches sang,
Ah, whence, and whither flown again, who knows!

QUATRAIN XI p. 84

[Second Edition of the Translation]

With me along the Strip of Herbage strown
That just divides the desert from the sown,
  Where name of Slave and Sultán is forgot—
And Peace to Máhmúd on his golden Throne?

QUATRAIN XX   p. 89

[Second Edition of the Translation]

The Palace that to Heav'n his pillars threw,
And Kings the forehead on his threshold drew—
    I saw the solitary Ringdove there,
And "Coo, coo, coo," she cried; and "Coo, coo, coo."

QUATRAIN XLIV p. 101

[*Second Edition of the Translation*]

Do you, within your little hour of Grace,
The waving Cypress in your Arms enlace,
  Before the Mother back into her arms
Fold, and dissolve you in a last embrace.

XXXVI

Earth could not answer: nor the Seas that mourn
In flowing Purple, of their Lord forlorn;
　　Nor Heaven, with those eternal Signs reveal'd
And hidden by the sleeve of Night and Morn.

XXXVII

Then of the THEE IN ME who works behind
The Veil of Universe I cried to find
　　A Lamp to guide me through the Darkness; and
Something then said—"An Understanding blind."

XXXVIII

Then to the Lip of this poor earthen Urn
I lean'd, the Secret Well of Life to learn:
    And Lip to Lip it murmur'd—"While you live,
Drink!—for, once dead, you never shall return."

XXXIX

I think the Vessel, that with fugitive
Articulation answer'd, once did live,
    And drink; and that impassive Lip I kiss'd,
How many Kisses might it take—and give!

XL

For I remember stopping by the way
To watch a Potter thumping his wet Clay:
   And with its all-obliterated Tongue
It murmur'd—"Gently, Brother, gently, pray!"

XLI

For has not such a Story from of Old
Down Man's successive generations roll'd
   Of such a clod of saturated Earth
Cast by the Maker into Human mould?

XLII

And not a drop that from our Cups we throw
On the parcht herbage but may steal below
   To quench the fire of Anguish in some Eye
There hidden—far beneath, and long ago.

XLIII

As then the Tulip for her wonted sup
Of Heavenly Vintage lifts her chalice up,
   Do you, twin offspring of the soil, till Heav'n
'To Earth invert you like an empty Cup.

XLIV

Do you, within your little hour of Grace,
The waving Cypress in your Arms enlace,
　　Before the Mother back into her arms
Fold, and dissolve you in a last embrace.

XLV

And if the Cup you drink, the Lip you press,
End in what All begins and ends in—Yes;
　　Imagine then you *are* what heretofore
You *were*—hereafter you shall not be less.

XLVI

So when at last the Angel of the drink
Of Darkness finds you by the river-brink,
   And, proffering his Cup, invites your Soul
Forth to your Lips to quaff it—do not shrink.

XLVII

And fear not lest Existence closing *your*
Account, should lose, or know the type no more;
   The Eternal Sákí from that Bowl has pour'd
Millions of Bubbles like us, and will pour.

XLVIII

When You and I behind the Veil are past,
Oh, but the long long while the World shall last,
   Which of our Coming and Departure heeds
As much as Ocean of a pebble-cast.

XLIX

One Moment in Annihilation's Waste,
One Moment, of the Well of Life to taste—
   The Stars are setting, and the Caravan
Draws to the Dawn of Nothing—Oh, make haste!

L

Would you that spangle of Existence spend
About THE SECRET—quick about it, Friend!
   A Hair, they say, divides the False and True—
And upon what, prithee, does Life depend?

LI

A Hair, they say, divides the False and True;
Yes; and a single Alif were the clue—
   Could you but find it, to the Treasure-house,
And peradventure to THE MASTER too;

LII

Whose secret Presence, through Creation's veins
Running, Quicksilver-like eludes your pains;
   Taking all shapes from Máh to Máhi; and
They change and perish all—but He remains;

LIII

A moment guess'd—then back behind the Fold
Immerst of Darkness round the Drama roll'd
   Which, for the Pastime of Eternity,
He does Himself contrive, enact, behold,

LIV

But if in vain, down on the stubborn floor
Of Earth, and up to Heav'n's unopening Door,
  You gaze To-DAY, while You are You—how then
To-MORROW, You when shall be You no more?

LV

Oh, plagued no more with Human or Divine,
To-morrow's tangle to itself resign,
  And lose your fingers in the tresses of
The Cypress-slender Minister of Wine.

LVI

Waste not your Hour, nor in the vain pursuit
Of This and That endeavour and dispute;
    Better be merry with the fruitful Grape
Than sadden after none, or bitter, Fruit.

LVII

You know, my Friends, how bravely in my House
For a new Marriage I did make Carouse;
    Divorced old barren Reason from my Bed,
And took the Daughter of the Vine to Spouse.

LVIII

For "Is" and "Is-NOT" though with Rule and Line,
And "UP-AND-DOWN" by Logic I define,
   Of all that one should care to fathom, I
Was never deep in anything but—Wine.

LIX

Ah, but my Computations, People say,
Have squared the Year to human compass, eh?
   If so, by striking from the Calendar
Unborn To-morrow, and dead Yesterday.

LX

And lately, by the Tavern Door agape,
Came shining through the Dusk an Angel Shape
   Bearing a Vessel on his Shoulder; and
He bid me taste of it; and 'twas—the Grape!

LXI

The Grape that can with Logic absolute
The Two-and-Seventy jarring Sects confute:
   The sovereign Alchemist that in a trice
Life's leaden metal into Gold transmute:

LXII

The mighty Mahmúd, Allah-breathing Lord,
That all the misbelieving and black Horde
    Of Fears and Sorrows that infest the Soul
Scatters before him with his whirlwind Sword.

LXIII

Why, be this Juice the growth of God, who dare
Blaspheme the twisted tendril as a Snare?
    A Blessing, we should use it, should we not?
And if a Curse—why, then, Who set it there?

LXIV

I must adjure the Balm of Life, I must,
Scared by some After-reckoning ta'en on trust,
   Or lured with Hope of some Diviner Drink,
When the frail Cup is crumbled into Dust!

LXV

If but the Vine and Love-adjuring Band
Are in the Prophet's Paradise to stand,
   Alack, I doubt the Prophet's Paradise
Were empty as the hollow of one's Hand.

LXVI

Oh, threats of Hell and Hopes of Paradise!
One thing at least is certain—*This* Life flies;
   One thing is certain and the rest is Lies;
The Flower that once is blown for ever dies.

LXVII

Strange, is it not? that of the myriads who
Before us pass'd the door of Darkness through,
   Not one returns to tell us of the Road,
Which to discover we must travel too.

LXVIII

The Revelations of Devout and Learn'd
Who rose before us, and as Prophets burn'd,
 Are all but Stories, which, awoke from Sleep
They told their fellows, and to Sleep return'd.

LXIX

Why, if the Soul can fling the Dust aside,
And naked on the Air of Heaven ride,
 Is't not a Shame—is't not a Shame for him
So long in this Clay suburb to abide!

LXX

But that is but a Tent wherein may rest
A Sultán to the realm of Death addrest;
    The Sultán rises, and the dark Ferrásh
Strikes, and prepares it for another Guest.

LXXI

I sent my Soul through the Invisible,
Some letter of that After-life to spell:
    And after many days my Soul return'd
And said, "Behold, Myself am Heav'n and Hell:"

LXXII

Heav'n but the Vision of fulfill'd Desire,
And Hell the Shadow of a Soul on fire,
    Cast on the Darkness into which Ourselves,
So late emerged from, shall so soon expire.

LXXIII

We are no other than a moving row
Of visionary Shapes that come and go
    Round with this Sun-illumined Lantern held
In Midnight by the Master of the Show;

LXXIV

Impotent Pieces of the Game He plays
Upon this Chequer-board of Nights and Days;
   Hither and thither moves, and checks, and slays,
And one by one back in the Closet lays.

LXXV

The Ball no question makes of Ayes and Noes,
But Right or Left as strikes the Player goes;
   And He that toss'd you down into the Field,
He knows about it all—HE knows—HE knows!

LXXVI

The Moving Finger writes; and, having writ,
Moves on: nor all your Piety nor Wit
   Shall lure it back to cancel half a Line,
Nor all your Tears wash out a Word of it.

LXXVII

For let Philosopher and Doctor preach
Of what they will, and what they will not—each
   Is but one Link in an eternal Chain
That none can slip, nor break, nor overreach.

LXXVIII

And that inverted Bowl we call The Sky,
Whereunder crawling coop'd we live and die,
   Lift not your hands to *It* for help—for It
As impotently rolls as you or I.

LXXIX

With Earth's first Clay They did the Last Man knead,
And there of the Last Harvest sow'd the Seed:
   And the first Morning of Creation wrote
What the Last Dawn of Reckoning shall read.

LXXX

Yesterday, *This* Day's Madness did prepare:
To-morrow's Silence, Triumph, or Despair:
    Drink! for you know not whence you came, nor why:
Drink! for you know not why you go, nor where.

LXXXI

I tell you this—When, started from the Goal,
Over the flaming shoulders of the Foal
    Of Heav'n Parwín and Mushtarí they flung,
In my predestined Plot of Dust and Soul.

LXXXII

The Vine had struck a fibre: which about
If clings my being—let the Dervish flout;
    Of my Base metal may be filed a Key,
That shall unlock the Door he howls without.

LXXXIII

And this I know: whether the one True Light
Kindle to Love, or Wrath-consume me quite,
    One Flash of It within the Tavern caught
Better than in the Temple lost outright.

LXXXIV

What! out of senseless Nothing to provoke
A conscious Something to resent the yoke
   Of unpermitted Pleasure, under pain
Of Everlasting Penalties, if broke!

LXXXV

What! from his helpless Creature be repaid
Pure Gold for what he lent us dross-allay'd
   Sue for a Debt we never did contract,
And cannot answer—Oh, the sorry trade!

LXXXVI

Nay, but, for terror of his wrathful Face,
I swear I will not call Injustice Grace;
    Not one Good Fellow of the Tavern but
Would kick so poor a Coward from the place.

LXXXVII

Oh, Thou, who didst with pitfall and with gin
Beset the Road I was to wander in,
    Thou wilt not with Predestined Evil round
Enmesh, and then impute my Fall to Sin!

LXXXVIII

Oh, Thou, who Man of baser Earth didst make,
And ev'n with Paradise devise the Snake:
   For all the Sin the Face of wretched Man
Is black with—Man's Forgiveness give—and take!

*   *   *   *   *

LXXXIX

As under cover of departing Day
Slunk hunger-stricken Ramazán away,
   Once more within the Potter's house alone
I stood, surrounded by the Shapes of Clay.

XC

And once again there gathered a scarce heard
Whisper among them; as it were, the stirr'd
   Ashes of some all but extinguisht Tongue,
Which mine ear kindled into living Word.

XCI

Said one among them—"Surely not in vain,
My substance from the common Earth was ta'en,
   That He who subtly wrought me into Shape
Should stamp me back to shapeless Earth again?"

XCII

Another said—"Why, ne'er a peevish Boy
Would break the Cup from which he drank in Joy;
   Shall He that of His own free Fancy made
The Vessel, in an after-rage destroy!"

XCIII

None answer'd this; but after silence spake
Some Vessel of a more ungainly Make;
   "They sneer at me for leaning all awry;
What! did the Hand then of the Potter shake?"

XCIV

Thus with the Dead as with the Living, *What?*
And *Why?* so ready, but the *Wherefor* not
    One on a sudden peevishly exclaim'd,
"Which is the Potter, pray, and which the Pot?"

XCV

Said one—"Folks of a surly Master tell,
And daub his Visage with the Smoke of Hell;
    They talk of some sharp Trial of us—Pish!
He's a Good Fellow, and 'twill all be well."

XCVI

"Well," said another, "Whoso will, let try,
  My Clay with long oblivion is gone dry:
    But fill me with the old familiar Juice,
  Methinks I might recover by-and-by!"

XCVII

So while the Vessels one by one were speaking,
One spied the little Crescent all were seeking:
    And then they jogg'd each other, "Brother! Brother!
Now for the Porter's shoulder-knot a-creaking!"

*   *   *   *   *

XCVIII

Ah, with the Grape my fading Life provide,
And wash my Body whence the Life has died,
  And lay me, shrouded in the living Leaf,
By some not unfrequented Garden-side.

XCIX

Whither resorting from the vernal Heat
Shall Old Acquaintance Old Acquaintance greet
  Under the Branch that leans above the Wall
To shed his Blossom over head and feet.

C

Then ev'n my buried Ashes such a snare
Of Vintage shall fling up into the Air,
   As not a True-believer passing by
But shall be overtaken unaware.

CI

Indeed the Idols I have loved so long
Have done my credit in Men's eye much wrong:
   Have drown'd my Glory in a shallow Cup
And sold my Reputation for a Song.

CII

Indeed, indeed, Repentance oft before
I swore—but was I sober when I swore?
   And then and then came Spring, and Rose-in-hand
My thread-bare Penitence apieces tore.

CIII

And much as Wine has play'd the Infidel,
And robb'd me of my Robe of Honour—Well,
   I often wonder what the Vintners buy
One-half so precious as the ware they sell.

CIV

Yet Ah, that Spring should vanish with the Rose!
That Youth's sweet-scented manuscript should close!
   The Nightingale that in the branches sang,
Ah, whence, and whither flown again, who knows!

CV

Would but the Desert of the Fountain yield
One glimpse—if dimly, yet indeed reveal'd,
   Toward which the fainting Traveller might spring,
As springs the trampled herbage of the field!

CVI

Oh, if the World were but to re-create,
That we might catch ere closed the Book of Fate,
    And make The Writer on a fairer leaf
Inscribe our names, or quite obliterate!

CVII

Better, oh, better, cancel from the Scroll
Of Universe one luckless Human Soul,
    Than drop by drop enlarge the Flood that rolls
Hoarser with Anguish as the Ages Roll.

CVIII

Ah, Love! could you and I with Fate conspire
To grasp this sorry Scheme of Things entire,
    Would not we shatter it to bits—and then
Re-mould it nearer to the Heart's Desire!

CIX

But see! The rising Moon of Heav'n again—
Looks for us, Sweet-heart, through the quivering Plane:
    How oft hereafter rising will she look
Among those leaves—for one of us in vain!

CX

And when Yourself with silver Foot shall pass
Among the Guests Star-scatter'd on the Grass,
   And in your joyous errand reach the spot
Where I made One—turn down an empty Glass!

TAMÁM

I

*W*AKE! For the Sun, who scatter'd into flight
The Stars before him from the Field of Night,
Drives Night along with them from Heav'n,
and strikes
The Sultán's Turret with a Shaft of Light.

II

Before the phantom of False morning died,
Methought a Voice within the Tavern cried,
 "When all the Temple is prepared within,
Why nods the drowsy Worshipper outside?"

III

And, as the Cock crew, those who stood before
The Tavern shouted—"Open then the Door!
 You know how little while we have to stay,
And, once departed, may return no more."

IV

Now the New Year reviving old Desires,
The thoughtful Soul to Solitude retires,
    Where the WHITE HAND OF MOSES on the Bough
Puts out, and Jesus from the Ground suspires.

V

Iram indeed is gone with all his Rose,
And Jamshýd's Sev'n-ring'd Cup where no one knows;
    But still a Ruby kindles in the Vine,
And many a Garden by the Water blows.

VI

And David's lips are lockt; but in divine
High-piping Pehleví, with "Wine! Wine! Wine!
   Red Wine!"—the Nightingale cries to the Rose
That sallow cheek of hers t' incarnadine.

VII

Come, fill the Cup, and in the fire of Spring
Your Winter-garment of Repentance fling:
   The Bird of Time has but a little way
To flutter—and the Bird is on the Wing.

VIII

Whether at Naishápúr or Babylon,
Whether the Cup with sweet or bitter run,
    The Wine of Life keeps oozing drop by drop,
The Leaves of Life keep falling one by one.

IX

Each Morn a thousand Roses brings, you say;
Yes, but where leaves the Rose of Yesterday?
    And this first Summer month that brings the Rose
Shall take Jamshýd and Kaikobád away.

X

Well, let it take them! What have we to do
With Kaikobád the Great, or Kaikhosrú?
    Let Zál and Rustum bluster as they will,
Or Hátim call to Supper—heed not you

XI

With me along the strip of Herbage strown
That just divides the desert from the sown,
    Where name of Slave and Sultán is forgot—
And Peace to Mahmúd on his golden Throne!

XII

A Book of Verses underneath the Bough,
A Jug of Wine, a Loaf of Bread—and Thou
    Beside me singing in the Wilderness—
Oh, Wilderness were Paradise enow!

XIII

Some for the Glories of This World; and some
Sigh for the Prophet's Paradise to come;
    Ah, take the Cash, and let the Credit go,
Nor heed the rumble of a distant Drum!

XIV

Look to the blowing Rose about us—"Lo,
Laughing," she says, "into the world I blow,
    At once the silken tassel of my Purse
Tear, and its Treasure on the Garden throw."

XV

And those who husbanded the Golden grain,
And those who flung it to the winds like Rain,
    Alike to no such aureate Earth are turn'd
As, buried once, Men want dug up again.

XVI

The Worldly Hope men set their Hearts upon
Turns Ashes—or it prospers; and anon,
   Like Snow upon the Desert's dusty Face,
Lighting a little hour or two—is gone.

XVII

Think, in this batter'd Caravanserai
Whose Portals are alternate Night and Day,
   How Sultán after Sultán with his Pomp
Abode his destined Hour, and went his way.

XVIII

They say the Lion and the Lizard keep
The Courts where Jamshýd gloried and drank deep:
   And Bahrám, that great Hunter—the Wild Ass
Stamps o'er his Head, but cannot break his Sleep.

XIX

I sometimes think that never blows so red
The Rose as where some buried Cæsar bled;
   That every Hyacinth the Garden wears
Dropt in her Lap from some once lovely Head.

QUATRAIN LXXII p. 115

[Second Edition of the Translation]

Heav'n but the Vision of fulfill'd Desire,
And Hell the Shadow of a Soul on fire,
 Cast on the Darkness into which Ourselves,
So late emerged from, shall so soon expire.

QUATRAIN XIV p. 142

[*Fifth Edition of the Translation*]

Look to the blowing Rose about us—"Lo,
Laughing," she says, "into the world I blow,
  At once the silken tassel of my Purse
Tear, and its Treasure on the Garden throw."

QUATRAIN XXXVII   p. 153

[Fifth Edition of the Translation]

For I remember stopping by the way
To watch a Potter thumping his wet Clay:
    And with its all-obliterated Tongue
It murmur'd—"Gently, Brother, gently, pray!"

QUATRAIN XLI p. 155

[*Fifth Edition of the Translation*]

Perplext no more with Human or Divine,
To-morrow's tangle to the winds resign,
    And lose your fingers in the tresses of
The Cypress-slender Minister of Wine.

XX

And this reviving Herb whose tender Green
Fledges the River-Lip on which we lean—
   Ah, lean upon it lightly! for who knows
From what once lovely Lip it springs unseen!

XXI

Ah, my Belovéd, fill the Cup that clears
To-DAY of Past Regrets and Future Fears:
   To-morrow!—Why, To-morrow I may be
Myself with Yesterday's Sev'n Thousand Years

XXII

For some we loved, the loveliest and the best
That from his Vintage rolling Time hath prest,
  Have drunk their Cup a Round or two before,
And one by one crept silently to rest.

XXIII

And we, that now make merry in the Room
They left, and Summer dresses in new bloom
  Ourselves must we beneath the Couch of Earth
Descend—ourselves to make a Couch—for whom?

XXIV

Ah, make the most of what we yet may spend,
Before we too into the Dust descend;
   Dust into Dust, and under Dust to lie
Sans Wine, sans Song, sans Singer, and—sans End!

XXV

Alike for those who for To-DAY prepare,
And those that after some To-MORROW stare,
   A Muezzín from the Tower of Darkness cries
"Fools! your Reward is neither Here nor There."

XXVI

Why, all the Saints and Sages who discuss'd
Of the Two Worlds so wisely—they are thrust
   Like foolish Prophets forth; their Words to Scorn
Are scatter'd, and their Mouths are stopt with Dust.

XXVII

Myself when young did eagerly frequent
Doctor and Saint, and heard great argument
   About it and about: but evermore
Came out by the same door where in I went.

XXVIII

With them the seed of Wisdom did I sow,
And with mine own hand wrought to make it grow;
   And this was all the Harvest that I reap'd—
"I came like Water, and like Wind I go."

XXIX

Into this Universe, and *Why* not knowing
Nor *Whence*, like Water willy-nilly flowing;
   And out of it, as Wind along the Waste,
I know not *Whither*, willy-nilly blowing.

XXX

What, without asking, hither hurried *Whence?*
And, without asking, *Whither* hurried hence!
   Oh, many a Cup of this forbidden Wine
Must drown the memory of that insolence!

XXXI

Up from Earth's Centre through the Seventh Gate
I rose, and on the Throne of Saturn sate;
   And many a Knot unravel'd by the Road;
But not the Master-knot of Human Fate.

XXXII

There was the Door to which I found no Key;
There was the Veil through which I might not see:
　　Some little talk awhile of Me and Thee
There was—and then no more of Thee and Me.

XXXIII

Earth could not answer; nor the Seas that mourn
In flowing Purple, of their Lord forlorn;
　　Nor rolling Heaven, with all his Signs reveal'd
And hidden by the sleeve of Night and Morn.

XXXIV

Then of the THEE in ME who works behind
The Veil, I lifted up my hands to find
    A Lamp amid the Darkness; and I heard,
As from Without—"THE ME WITHIN THEE BLIND!"

XXXV

Then to the lip of this poor earthen Urn
I lean'd, the Secret of my Life to learn:
    And Lip to Lip it murmur'd—"While you live
Drink!—for, once dead, you never shall return."

XXXVI

I think the Vessel, that with fugitive
Articulation answer'd, once did live,
    And drink; and Ah! the passive Lip I kiss'd,
How many Kisses might it take—and give!

XXXVII

For I remember stopping by the way
To watch a Potter thumping his wet Clay:
    And with its all-obliterated Tongue
It murmur'd—"Gently, Brother, gently, pray!"

XXXVIII

And has not such a Story from of Old
Down Man's successive generations roll'd
   Of such a clod of saturated Earth
Cast by the Maker into Human mould?

XXXIX

And not a drop that from our Cups we throw
For Earth to drink of, but may steal below
   To quench the fire of Anguish in some Eye
There hidden—far beneath, and long ago.

XL

As then the Tulip for her morning sup
Of Heav'nly Vintage from the soil looks up,
 Do you devoutly do the like, till Heav'n
To Earth invert you—like an empty Cup.

XLI

Perplext no more with Human or Divine,
To-morrow's tangle to the winds resign,
 And lose your fingers in the tresses of
The Cypress-slender Minister of Wine.

XLII

And if the Wine you drink, the Lip you press
End in what All begins and ends in—Yes;
  Think then you are To-day what Yesterday
You were—To-morrow you shall not be less.

XLIII

So when that Angel of the darker Drink
At last shall find you by the river-brink,
  And, offering his Cup, invite your Soul
Forth to your Lips to quaff—you shall not shrink.

XLIV

Why, if the Soul can fling the Dust aside,
And naked on the Air of Heaven ride,
   Were't not a Shame—were't not a Shame for him
In this clay carcase crippled to abide?

XLV

'Tis but a Tent where takes his one day's rest
A Sultán to the realm of Death addrest;
   The Sultán rises, and the dark Ferrásh
Strikes, and prepares it for another Guest.

XLVI

And fear not lest Existence closing your
Account, and mine, should know the like no more;
   The Eternal Sákí from that Bowl has pour'd
Millions of Bubbles like us, and will pour.

XLVII

When You and I behind the Veil are past,
Oh, but the long, long while the World shall last,
   Which of our Coming and Departure heeds
As the Sea's self should heed a pebble-cast.

XLVIII

A Moment's Halt—a momentary taste
Of BEING from the Well amid the Waste—
   And Lo!—the phantom Caravan has reach'd
The NOTHING it set out from—Oh, make haste!

XLIX

Would you that spangle of Existence spend
About THE SECRET—quick about it, Friend!
   A Hair perhaps divides the False and True—
And upon what, prithee, may life depend?

L

A Hair perhaps divides the False and True;
Yes; and a single Alif were the clue—
   Could you but find it—to the Treasure-house,
And peradventure to THE MASTER too;

LI

Whose secret Presence, through Creation's veins
Running Quicksilver-like eludes your pains;
   Taking all shapes from Máh to Máhi; and
They change and perish all—but He remains;

LII

A moment guess'd—then back behind the Fold
Immerst of Darkness round the Drama roll'd
   Which, for the Pastime of Eternity,
He doth Himself contrive, enact, behold.

LIII

But if in vain, down on the stubborn floor
Of Earth, and up to Heav'n's unopening Door
   You gaze To-DAY, while You are You—how then
To-MORROW, You when shall be You no more?

LIV

Waste not your Hour, nor in the vain pursuit
Of This and That endeavour and dispute;
   Better be jocund with the fruitful Grape
Than sadden after none, or bitter, Fruit.

LV

You know, my Friends, with what a brave Carouse
I made a Second Marriage in my house;
   Divorced old barren Reason from my Bed
And took the Daughter of the Vine to Spouse.

LVI

For "Is" and "Is-NOT" though with Rule and Line
And "UP-AND-DOWN" by Logic I define,
   Of all that one should care to fathom, I
Was never deep in anything but—Wine.

LVII

Ah, but my Computations, People say,
Reduced the Year to better reckoning?—Nay
   'Twas only striking from the Calendar
Unborn To-morrow, and dead Yesterday.

LVIII

And lately, by the Tavern Door agape,
Came shining through the Dusk an Angel Shape
   Bearing a Vessel on his Shoulder; and
He bid me taste of it; and 'twas—the Grape!

LIX

The Grape that can with Logic absolute
The Two-and-Seventy jarring Sects confute:
   The sovereign Alchemist that in a trice
Life's leaden metal into Gold transmute:

LX

The mighty Mahmúd, Allah-breathing Lord
That all the misbelieving and black Horde
    Of Fears and Sorrows that infest the Soul
Scatters before him with his whirlwind Sword.

LXI

Why, be this Juice the growth of God, who dare
Blaspheme the twisted tendril as a Snare?
    A Blessing, we should use it, should we not?
And if a Curse—why, then, Who set it there?

LXII

I must abjure the Balm of Life, I must,
Scared by some After-reckoning ta'en on trust,
   Or lured with Hope of some Diviner Drink,
To fill the Cup—when crumbled into Dust!

LXIII

Oh, threats of Hell and Hopes of Paradise!
One thing at least is certain—*This* Life flies;
   One thing is certain and the rest is Lies;
The Flower that once has blown for ever dies.

LXIV

Strange, is it not? that of the myriads who
Before us pass'd the door of Darkness through,
   Not one returns to tell us of the Road,
Which to discover we must travel too.

LXV

The Revelations of Devout and Learn'd
Who rose before us, and as Prophets burn'd,
   Are all but Stories, which, awoke from Sleep,
They told their comrades, and to Sleep return'd.

LXVI

I sent my Soul through the Invisible,
Some letter of that After-life to spell:
   And by and by my Soul return'd to me,
And answer'd "I Myself am Heav'n and Hell:"

LXVII

Heav'n but the Vision of fulfill'd Desire,
And Hell the Shadow from a Soul on fire,
   Cast on the Darkness into which Ourselves,
So late emerged from, shall so soon expire.

LXVIII

We are no other than a moving row
Of Magic Shadow-shapes that come and go
    Round with the Sun-illumined Lantern held
In Midnight by the Master of the Show;

LXIX

But helpless Pieces of the Game He plays
Upon this Chequer-board of Nights and Days;
    Hither and thither moves, and checks, and slays,
And one by one back in the Closet lays.

LXX

The Ball no question makes of Ayes and Noes,
But Here or There as strikes the Player goes;
   And He that toss'd you down into the Field,
He knows about it all—HE knows—HE knows!

LXXI

The Moving Finger writes; and, having writ,
Moves on: nor all your Piety nor Wit
   Shall lure it back to cancel half a Line,
Nor all your Tears wash out a Word of it.

LXXII

And that inverted Bowl they call the Sky,
Whereunder crawling coop'd we live and die,
    Lift not your hands to *It* for help—for It
As impotently moves as you or I.

LXXIII

With Earth's first Clay They did the Last Man knead,
And there of the Last Harvest sow'd the Seed:
    And the first Morning of Creation wrote
What the Last Dawn of Reckoning shall read.

LXXIV

YESTERDAY *This* Day's Madness did prepare;
To-MORROW's Silence, Triumph, or Despair:
    Drink! for you know not whence you came, nor why:
Drink! for you know not why you go, nor where.

LXXV

I tell you this—When, started from the Goal,
Over the flaming shoulders of the Foal
    Of Heav'n Parwín and Mushtarí they flung
In my predestined Plot of Dust and Soul.

LXXVI

The Vine had struck a fibre: which about
If clings my being—let the Dervish flout;
   Of my Base metal may be filed a Key,
That shall unlock the Door he howls without.

LXXVII

And this I know: whether the one True Light
Kindle to Love, or Wrath-consume me quite,
   One Flash of It within the Tavern caught
Better than in the Temple lost outright.

LXXVIII

What! out of senseless Nothing to provoke
A conscious Something to resent the yoke
   Of unpermitted Pleasure, under pain
Of Everlasting Penalties, if broke!

LXXIX

What! from his helpless Creature be repaid
Pure Gold for what he lent him dross-allay'd—
   Sue for a Debt he never did contract,
And cannot answer—Oh, the sorry trade!

LXXX

Oh, Thou, who didst with pitfall and with gin
Beset the Road I was to wander in,
    Thou wilt not with Predestined Evil round
Enmesh, and then impute my Fall to Sin!

LXXXI

Oh, Thou, who Man of baser Earth didst make,
And ev'n with Paradise devise the Snake:
    For all the Sin wherewith the Face of Man
Is blacken'd—Man's forgiveness give—and take!

*   *   *   *   *

LXXXII

As under cover of departing Day
Slunk hunger-stricken Ramazán away,
 Once more within the Potter's house alone
I stood, surrounded by the Shapes of Clay.

LXXXIII

Shapes of all Sorts and Sizes, great and small,
That stood along the floor and by the wall;
 And some loquacious Vessels were; and some
Listen'd perhaps, but never talk'd at all.

LXXXIV

Said one among them—"Surely not in vain
My substance of the common Earth was ta'en
   And to this Figure moulded, to be broke,
Or trampled back to shapeless Earth again."

LXXXV

Then said a Second—"Ne'er a peevish Boy
Would break the Bowl from which he drank in joy,
   And He that with his hand the Vessel made
Will surely not in after Wrath destroy."

LXXXVI

After a momentary silence spake
Some Vessel of a more ungainly Make;
   "They sneer at me for leaning all awry:
What! did the Hand then of the Potter shake?"

LXXXVII

Whereat some one of the loquacious Lot—
I think a Súfi pipkin—waxing hot—
   "All this of Pot and Potter—Tell me then,
Who is the Potter, pray, and who the Pot?"

LXXXVIII

"Why," said another, "Some there are who tell
Of one who threatens he will toss to Hell
    The luckless Pots he marr'd in making—Pish!
He's a Good Fellow, and 'twill all be well."

LXXXIX

"Well," murmur'd one, "Let whoso make or buy,
My Clay with long Oblivion is gone dry:
    But fill me with the old familiar Juice,
Methinks I might recover by and by."

XC

So while the Vessels one by one were speaking,
The little Moon look'd in that all were seeking:
   And then they jogg'd each other, "Brother! Brother!
Now for the Porter's shoulder-knot a-creaking!"

         *   *   *   *   *

XCI

Ah, with the Grape my fading Life provide,
And wash the Body whence the Life has died,
   And lay me, shrouded in the living Leaf,
By some not unfrequented Garden-side.

XCII

That ev'n my buried Ashes such a snare
Of Vintage shall fling up into the Air
    As not a True-believer passing by
But shall be overtaken unaware.

XCIII

Indeed the Idols I have loved so long
Have done my credit in this World much wrong:
    Have drown'd my Glory in a shallow Cup
And sold my Reputation for a Song.

XCIV

Indeed, indeed, Repentance oft before
I swore—but was I sober when I swore?
    And then and then came Spring, and Rose-in-hand
My thread-bare Penitence apieces tore.

XCV

And much as Wine has play'd the Infidel,
And robb'd me of my Robe of Honour—Well,
    I wonder often what the Vintners buy
One half so precious as the stuff they sell.

XCVI

Yet Ah, that Spring should vanish with the Rose!
That Youth's sweet-scented manuscript should close!
    The Nightingale that in the branches sang,
Ah, whence, and whither flown again, who knows!

XCVII

Would but the Desert of the Fountain yield
One glimpse—if dimly, yet indeed, reveal'd,
    To which the fainting Traveller might spring,
As springs the trampled herbage of the field!

XCVIII

Would but some wingéd Angel ere too late
Arrest the yet unfolded Roll of Fate,
    And make the stern Recorder otherwise
Enregister, or quite obliterate!

XCIX

Ah, Love! could you and I with Him conspire
To grasp this sorry Scheme of Things entire,
    Would not we shatter it to bits—and then
Re-mould it nearer to the Heart's Desire!

*   *   *   *   *

C

Yon rising Moon that looks for us again—
How oft hereafter will she wax and wane;
   How oft hereafter rising look for us
Through this same Garden—and for *one* in vain!

CI

And when like her, oh, Sákí, you shall pass
Among the Guests Star-scatter'd on the Grass,
   And in your joyous errand reach the spot
Where I made One—turn down an empty Glass!

TAMAM

VARIATIONS IN

THE THIRD EDITION

OF THE TRANSLATION

In the first draught of the Third Edition the first quatrain stood thus:

W AKE! For the Sun before him into Night
A signal flung that put the Stars to flight;
    And, to the field of Heav'n ascending, strikes
The Sultán's Turret with a Shaft of Light.

*The tenth quatrain read thus in the
Third Edition:*

Well, let it take them! What have we to do
With Kaikobád the Great, or Kaikhosrú?
   Let Zál and Rustum thunder as they will,
Or Hátim Tai "To supper!"—heed not you.

*In the first draught of Third Edition the
thirty-eighth verse was as follows:*

For, in your Ear a moment—of the same
Poor Earth from which that Human whisper came,
   The luckless Mould in which Mankind was cast
They did compose, and call'd him by the name.

In the final draught of the Third Edition it was changed to read:

Listen—a moment listen!—Of the same
Poor Earth from which that Human Whisper came,
   The luckless Mould in which Mankind was cast
They did compose, and call'd him by the name.

In the first draught of Third Edition quatrain forty ran thus:

As then the Tulip from her wonted sup
Of Wine from Heav'n her little Tass lifts up,
   Do you, twin offspring of the soil, till Heav'n
To Earth invert you like an empty cup.

The first draught of the Third Edition carried quatrain forty-two as follows:

And if the Cup, and if the Lip you press,
End in what All begins and ends in—Yes;
    Imagine then you *are* what heretofore
You *were*—hereafter you shall not be less.

Quatrain forty-eight in the first draught of Third Edition read:

A Moment's Halt—a momentary taste
Of BEING from the Well amid the Waste—
    Before the starting Caravan has reach'd
The Nothing it set out from—Oh, make haste!

In the final draught of Third Edition the same stanza ran:

A Moment's Halt—a momentary taste
Of BEING from the Well amid the Waste—
    And Lo!—the phantom Caravan has reach'd
The Nothing it set out from—Oh, make haste!

In the first draught of the Third Edition, there stood the following quatrain, later deleted:

Better, oh, better, cancel from the Scroll
Of Universe one luckless Human Soul,
    Than drop by drop enlarge the Flood that rolls
Hoarser with Anguish as the Ages Roll.